But the fruit of the Spirit is love, joy, peace, patience, kindness, goodness, faithfulness, gentleness, self-control. Against such things there is no law.
— Galatians 5: 22-23 (NASB)

the Fruit of the Spirit

The **fruit of the Spirit,**

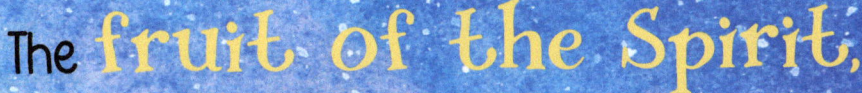

nine gifts we receive,

From the God who loves us, and in whom we believe.

Each one is a treasure, a blessing to share,

To show the world, that God's love is there.

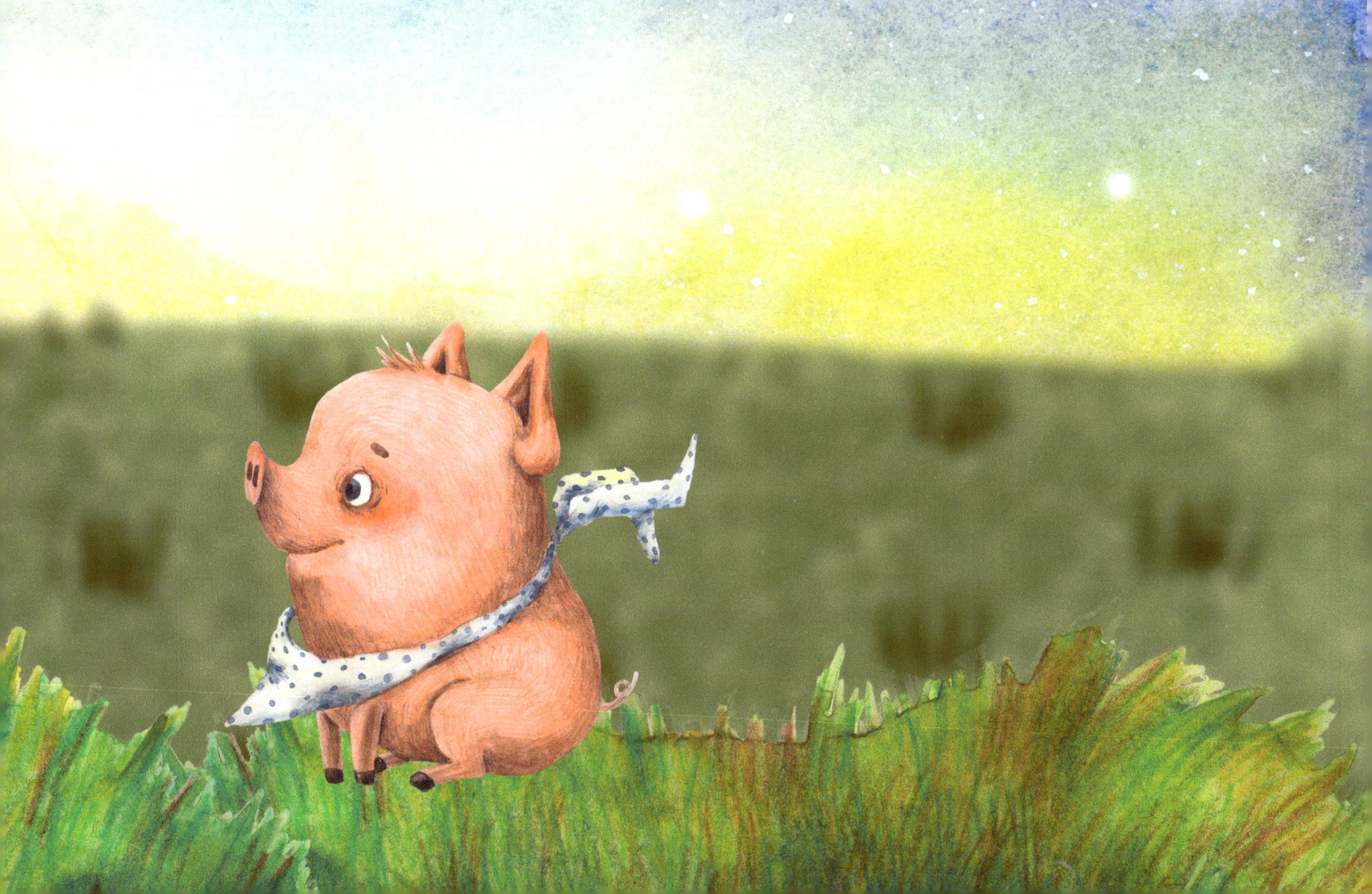

Love is the first, the greatest of all,
It covers all things, the big and the small.

It gives and forgives, it's patient and kind,
And keeps us close, in heart and in mind.

Joy is the gift,
that bubbles within,
It comes from knowing,
we're forgiven our sin.

It fills us with gladness,
and lightens our way,
And helps us to see,
a brighter new day.

Peace is the gift, that calms all our fear,
It reminds us, that God is always near.
It quiets our heart, and stills our soul,
And helps us to trust the One who's in control.

Patience is the gift, that helps us to wait,
It reminds us that things will come in their date.
It trusts in God's perfect timing,
And keeps our hearts from ever whining.

Kindness is the gift, that shows us the way,
To love and to serve, each and every day.
It gives us the eyes, to see others' needs,
And prompts us to act, on kind-hearted deeds.

Goodness is the gift, that shines from within,
It's the life we live when we turn from our sin.
It reflects God's love, in all that we do,
And helps us to grow, in grace, love, and truth.

Faithfulness is the promise that's kept,
The vow that's made and never left.
It stands through trials and through fears,
And shows God's love throughout the years.

Gentleness is the gift,
that touches the heart,
It's the way we love,
and the way we impart.
It helps us to see,
the value of all,
And leads us to help,
both the great and the small.

Self-control is the gift, that guides from within,
That helps us choose what's right - not sin.
It keeps us strong and focused too,
And leads us to grow, in God's love anew.

So let us strive to bear this fruit,
And let God's love shine through us too.
For when we do, the world will see,
The love of God, through you and me.

Dear Reader,

I hope that this book has brought a smile to your face! If you and your child have enjoyed reading it, I kindly ask that you take a moment to leave an honest rating and review on Amazon. Your feedback can help other readers find and enjoy the book as well.

If you're interested in exploring more of our publications, please check out our other books on Amazon by searching for Author Adoria Alina Maiyer Publishing. We appreciate your support and hope to continue bringing joy to your reading experiences.

Thank you!!!

Adoria

www.ingramcontent.com/pod-product-compliance
Lightning Source LLC
Chambersburg PA
CBHW041450120626
46547CB00002B/404